THE WAY BACK

Wyn Cooper

White Pine Press · Buffalo, New York

Acknowledgments
Agni: "The Life of the Mind." *American Literary Review:* "Firenze," "Holiday," "Twilight." *Denver Quarterly:* "Grind the Coffee," "Last Night." *Ellipsis:* "Natalia." *Elvis in Oz:* "On Eight Mile." *Fence:* "Oh See Disorder." *Great Stream Review:* "The Wonders." *Harvard Magazine:* "Vicious." *Hollins Critic:* "Frosting." *The Journal:* "Forty Words for Fear." *Marlboro Review:* "Chinese Lanterns." *Night Out:* "Bad Manners." *Pacific International:* "Fairy Tale." *Ploughshares:* "Puritan Impulse," "Talk." *Potash Hill:* "The Way Back," "Train." *Quarterly West:* "Gaposis," "Junkyard," "Kids," "Leaving the Country." *Verse:* "Confluence."

I would like to thank the Ucross Foundation, as well as Laure-Anne Bosselaar and Kurt Brown, for providing me with idyllic places to write, in Wyoming and France.

For close readings of my poems, suggestions, and support, I wish to thank Liam Rector, Shawna Parker, Ralph Wilson, Penelope Austin, Chris Merrill, Scott Cairns, the late Larry Levis, Valerie Duff, Amy Bottke, Joe Mueller, and John Strayer.

For help with the object you hold in your hands, I would like to thank Dennis Maloney, Elaine LaMattina, Anthony Cafritz, and Susan Lippman.

For permission to reprint "White Voodoo," from *Dissolving Clouds: Writings of Peter Hutchinson*, I wish to thank Peter Hutchinson, as well as Chris Busa of Provincetown Arts Press.

Finally, I would like to thank Tom Trusky and Ahsahta Press for permission to reprint "Fun" from my first book, *The Country of Here Below.*

Publication of this book was made possible, in part, by a grant from the New York State Council on the Arts.

Printed and bound in the United States of America.
Published by White Pine Press, P.O. Box 236, Buffalo, NY 14201.

Cover: "Split Development" by Anthony Cafritz. Photo by Wyn Cooper.

Library of Congress Cataloging-in-Publication Data
Cooper, Wyn 1957 –
The way back / Wyn Cooper.
p.cm.
ISBN 1-893996-03-4
I. Title.
PS3553.O628 W39 2000
811'.54—dc21   99-044071

▲

The Way Back

▼

CONTENTS

▲

MANNERS

▼

▲

TALK

▼

for my friends
▼
and for Shawna

▲
The Way Back
▼

White Voodoo

A few years ago I was walking through Central Park at 3 a.m. on 96th Street. There was a paper bag on the sidewalk and as I passed it I gave it a kick. Walking on, I thought that the sound I heard when I kicked the bag was like money. Hesitating, I went back and picked up the bag and opened it. Inside I found 60 cents in change and a white dove with its head cut off. The head was in there as well. I thought it must be some kind of voodoo. But since I was very broke at the time I used the money to buy breakfast the next morning. Since then things have gone very well for me.

—Peter Hutchinson,
from *Dissolving Clouds*

▲
Manners
▼

On Eight Mile

She appears as if at the edge
of a screen, her brown hair black
in this light, her legs moving the way

she wants you to want them to move.
It's hard to see the woman you loved
dance naked in a room full of men

and come up to your table after
and ask for a light, and the light
in her eyes is still the same,

only her job has changed. So she changes
into clothes and we cross the street
to a quiet place where we can talk,

and the talk turns to me, to what
I do that makes me think I'm better
than her. I'm not and I know it,

but she won't be convinced. Nothing
I can say will sway her the way
she sways on stage. And nothing

can make me look away.

Firenze

The women have all gone
to Italy. The men
have been left behind.

The women have gone to see
what the men would have
kept from them, which the men

can no longer have, now
that the women have gone
to a country shaped like a boot.

The men kick themselves with the boot
in their heads, where it hurts most.
At dawn they look into the sun,
toward the ocean across which
the women have flown.

The women are in Firenze. They burn
in the midday sun, and they will
burn tonight. The men continue
to say "Florence," and wonder
why they were left behind.

Your Ways

When is loud too loud,
chainsaw cutting words
you try to say in half,

heavy metal next door,
heavy people you can't
ask to turn it down,

child screaming bright red
Stop, sounds that pierce
more than your ears,

more than two ways
to skin a cat, but
what did you expect?

You moved here aware
of the volume of spite
and who's to judge that,

not someone who grew
up elsewhere, duly
elected, busy collecting

places like this, mental
pictures with descriptions
to match, paragraphs

on the back of your tongue
telling what you think,
don't speak or they might

go away, go back where
they were before you landed,
before they knew your ways.

Holiday

Speak not of the weather, dear,
but of whether or not we shall dance
on this fine August evening, bombs
falling nearby, guns in the streets,
the sun going down through a haze
of smoke and dust, and thunder
that won't go away.

　　　　　　So we'll go away,
we'll go sway for awhile, if we're allowed,
on an island of green in a sea of blue,
where waves like dogs lick the shore by day,
and by night fade out that we may sleep.

Don't mention how fine the wine is not,
or the food, or the band, because we
can go, this little war can't keep us here,
a little man with little boots
means nothing to me, and still less
to my country, which knows what to do.

The band is worse than ever—the drummer
has only one stick. My wine's too warm
and yours is gone. The man to your left
is bleeding, though his jaw is set
against concern. He must be one of ours.

Bad Manners

Guys with names like 8-Ball
live in this bar. The songs on the box
might sound familiar somewhere else,
but here they're dirty, almost
not sound at all. They blend in
to the other noises, the bottles,
the voices, the toilet that's flushed
only when someone
doesn't want to be heard.

As the night sails away
the patrons float above the floor,
as if to touch the ground
would be bad manners. Touch
of any kind is wrong—
it happens only in fights
and when money changes hands,
changes into something more
comfortable, wait here, I'll be
right back, watch my drink, don't
let it spill on the floor.

Last Night

Last night I ate steak
with a woman named Catfish.
Words flew around our heads,
wine spilled in our laps.
The meat reeked of another
world; it slid from our hands.

I lay down in a field
where a circus had been.
An earring cut my neck.
Red dogs licked my face awake.
I did not know left from right.

A Hundred Acres of Hate

crowned at the top of the long green hill
by a barn once red, now gray as it
sways to the north northeast, a barn
filled to the rafters with spite, on fire

in the mind of the man who lives here,
not a farmer, just someone who wants
to hear and see nothing of the rest
of the rest of the world, his mind astray

and happy that way, alone on the hill
looking down to the valley where now
and then he goes, walking the walk
he's always wanted, limp of the recluse

on unhallowed ground, the wuthering
heights of the mind matched only
by the depths to which the body sinks,
links in a chain around his neck.

—for Liam Rector

Twilight

Behind this barn two men are fighting,
taking turns putting fist to jaw.
They roll in the garden, killing the harvest,
then stand and gasp and start again.

Behind this barn the sun is setting
a little earlier every day.
The last light hits the tops of trees,
and soon they will fight in the dark.

The argument is over money. Neither man
has very much. The clouds to the west
are yellow and gold, bigger than mountains.
The men's faces are red, from anger, from blood.

Behind this barn, at twilight, in a state
far from clarity, two men can be seen
hugging each other like long lost friends.
They stand like shadows in shadowless light.

And now, again, they fight.

Chinese Lanterns

Peppers and onions piled in the sink
soon to be washed, chopped, tossed
on the grill, flavors released
one to the other, flesh
skin and seed, red yellow green,
the smell of loam not quite cooked out,

the cookout a success, the guests
dressed to eat, gathered in the yard
pretending to care, staring
each other down, then up, heads
bobbing like Chinese lanterns
casting blades of light on the grass

on which the guests begin to dance,
as if on the edge of a knife,
cutting to the quick, easy way home.

Gaposis

noun. Informal. 1. A noticeable gap or series of gaps between buttoned buttons or closed snaps on a garment when worn, as when the fabric is stretched out of shape around the fasteners; 2. A synthetic commercialism; 3. From *Walk in the Sun:* I'm anti-social...I got gap-osis; 4. From *Nuclear War: Gaposis* describes the American public's historical sensitivity to claims of U.S. nuclear inferiority...a missile gap, a bomber gap, an ABM gap, and a window of vulnerability.

Something is bursting the seams of the fabric
that contains all we hold dear,
that holds it in, shapes it,
gives it a life it might

not have known—clothes make us,
after all, into something we're not—
stretching the wool over our eyes,
only to take it away:

the self under spotlights, walking
the runway, waifs waiting
in the wings to fly onto and under
the covers of glossies, vague

is in vogue, what are you in? And
who do you want to look like today,
a man, a woman, a manta ray
ready to sting when styles change.

Dive to the bottom of the deep
blue crinoline cape
that waits for you, wrapped
around someone you thought you knew.

What does gingham say to you?
Elly Mae by the cement pond?
Jethro coming out of her closet,
shades of scarlett conquering?

Don't think of yourself, it's not
about you, it's a concept
clothed as a theory—all
dressed up and no one to be.

—for Anthony Cafritz

Talk

Puritan Impulse

I talk the least
of what I covet
most, seldom look
at what I wish to see,
turn my nose away
from what smells best,
refuse to listen
to my favorite opera,
La Traviata,
even when it's sung
in town for free.
The Van Gogh show
can't make me walk
the block to view it,
no chef can intuit
what I might want,
and handing me jars
of caviar while
popping Veuve Clicquot
is not what I call love.

The rain last night
froze on the birches,
and today they bend
almost to breaking.
The sun makes every
branch distinct, too bright
to look at for long.
And that's excuse
enough for me
to look back down
to the road
I walk on, ice
on the pavement
so clear it's blue.

Oh See Disorder

Heathenmobiles made of rust and sin
roar past my window. When
their noise has gone I hear my neighbor
talk to God, mostly of the weather
here, too shy to ask about it there.
I would ask, if He would answer,
but I'm not sure His mind is clean.

I leave my home, go downtown,
don't turn around when called a name
I quietly love, then I take
this job and love it too, the sweeping
and dusting, the putting in place
for no one to see, the making
quiet of that which is loud,
beguiling, the lying to others
about what I do: not this.

—for Tree Swenson

Junkyard

I built this junkyard
from nothing but hills rolling
in wheat and alfalfa. I wanted the hills

covered by cars of all
colors, fence to fence, two or
three high, rows and rows that would waver

in the sun like wheat
in Kansas wind. Some nights
I drove three hundred miles for a make

and a year I didn't have,
and some days they came to me.
I never took a car that didn't have a story—

why pay money for metal
and rubber, a body without a name?
Then I saw it, and I had to keep them.

I took another job,
one I still have and still hate,
so I can come home in late afternoon and walk

out among the stories
of wrong turns and say I saw it coming
from across these fields, a blue humming globe,

a small hollow planet
that floated just above the cars.
It was drawn to them, but was able to leave.

People come to hear the story.
One man said it was the only thing
that ever happened in my life, and that I made it up.

I tell you he's wrong.
It happened on the fifth of July,
and I hadn't been drinking. It happened fast,

blue light moving toward me,
going solid, growing, a humming
I'll never forget, a feeling I still have.

I have seen something
no one else has seen. I could change
the facts—people will believe me or they won't.

We change as quickly
as our words, so I use the same ones
to tell myself again what happened. No detail

has been changed, no fact
deleted. I'm as true to my story
as to my ruined cars, which sparkle now

after a light rain.

Postcard

Wish I could paint it, this sky out my window,
then you could see it the way I do now.

But it's fading, the sunset, as clouds move
across sky, as you move through love

on another coast, three time zones away,
three hours before the end of a day

during which you won't think of me once,
not my name, not my hands, not even my face

which you once loved to kiss, or so you said.
I managed to keep you drunk and well fed,

which was all you wanted when we met.
How far you've come, how quickly you went.

The Bureau of Alcohol, Tobacco, and Firearms

It rises right out of the ground, this feeling I get,
it comes through my feet and goes all the way up.
And then I don't know what I'm doing,
though I know I like it, and that's what
gets me later, a head full of guilt.
I'm sorry for everything, after it's done.

What I do most days is this: go down
to the store for a six-pack and smokes.
Come home, consume, get out my guns.
What happens after that is out of my hands.

I load a pistol, get back in the car,
and go for more beer. I swagger
into convenience stores, my dominion.
No one asks my gun's opinion.

Kids

A tincture of this, a spot of that
and I'm ready to go, down the stairs
and onto the streets, beyond the world
I live in, the one that bores me.

Tonight the kids are out in force.
I know they outnumber me, but
their cruelty depends on their boredom:
I try and try to make them laugh.

Past boredom lies horror, the kind
that wakes us up at night, a dream
too bad to sleep through. And *too bad*
is what they yell when I tell them it hurts.

They kick until the crack of bone,
the sight of blood that makes them leave.
I lie on the street and stare at the moon,
two hundred thirty eight thousand

miles away.

Talk

You're going to ask me why I am
here, and I'm going to tell you.
But I want you to look at the scar
on my arm, this one right here in the shape
of a mouth, though not a human one.
I like to talk about my scars, I like to talk

about all kinds of things, but there's no one to talk
to most of the time. Wherever I am
I watch, smell the air, don't sleep, I'm the one
who listens to the crazies, I listen to you
when you look out the window, talking to shapes
the snow makes in the yard, covering scars.

When you ask what that sound is I say it's cars,
can't you see them, but instead of talk
you give me a gaze, a look in the shape
of how we might look together, and I am
sinking, and trying not to, sinking toward you
down there on the floor, looking up, the One.

This is the way one gets to two, one
foot then the other, one hand on my scar,
waltzing around the kitchen with you,
the music, the music, no need to talk
of what this means to anyone, or why I am
here, the shadow on the wall a miraculous shape.

I can see in your mind a thought taking shape.
If only you could speak, you'd be the one
I came to get, to take away, but I am
sorry, I was wrong, I'll cover my scar
and leave you here, I won't try to talk
to anyone tonight, not me and not you.

Just two questions before I go: Do you
know how I got this scar? Is its shape
familiar? Come on, come on please talk
to me, tell me you bit me, say you're the one
who left a mark on my arm, a little scar
to remember you by, I'm asking you, I'm

begging, good God I'm pleading, you're the only one
who knows if it's a scar in the shape
of what you would say if you would talk.

Fun

"All I want is to have a little fun
Before I die," says the man next to me
Out of nowhere, apropos of nothing. He says
His name's William but I'm sure he's Bill
Or Billy, Mac or Buddy; he's plain ugly to me,
And I wonder if he's ever had fun in his life.

We are drinking beer at noon on Tuesday,
In a bar that faces a giant car wash.
The good people of the world are washing their cars
On their lunch hours, hosing and scrubbing
As best they can in skirts and suits.
They drive their shiny Datsuns and Buicks
Back to the phone company, the record store,
The genetic engineering lab, but not a single one
Appears to be having fun like Billy and me.

I like a good beer buzz early in the day,
And Billy likes to peel the labels
From his bottles of Bud and shred them on the bar.
Then he lights every match in an oversized pack,
Letting each one burn down to his thick fingers
Before blowing and cursing them out.

A happy couple enters the bar, dangerously close
To one another, like this is a motel,
But they clean up their act when we give them
A Look. One quick beer and they're out,
Down the road and in the next state
For all I care, smiling like idiots.
We cover sports and politics and once,
When Billy burns his thumb and lets out a yelp,
The bartender looks up from his want-ads.

Otherwise the bar is ours, and the day and the night
And the car wash too, the matches and the Buds
And the clean and dirty cars, the sun and the moon
And every motel on this highway. It's ours, you hear?
And we've got plans, so relax and let us in—
All we want is to have a little fun.

Dish

The deepest dish is served to those
who need it most, and woe betide
any who deign to disbelieve.
The rules are set in ink as blue
as the blood which made them,
the ache of thought and word,
believed or not, relieved of that
found most foul, eye-wide owl
hooting loud the question "Who?"

And who today dares go there,
the underbelly unzipped,
who will stare in that dark pit?
The people here, that's who.
The ones who want to eat you.

▲
What Might Fly Away
▼

Then there is a time in life when you just take a walk:
And you walk in your own landscape.

—Willem de Kooning

Leaving the Country

He drifts into a room of strangers
who tell stories he thinks he's heard
though they seem different this time,
more lurid and real. He's never seen
these people before, who seem to know
when to use the right word, when to drop
their voices to whispers, to say
the last time he came into this room
is the last time he went anywhere
and our man wants out, but must stay.

Each story takes the shape of a square
which works its way around him
until he's almost framed, then
he steps out, leaving a maze
of open squares all over the room
which itself is a square left open
at the door. He tries to shut
these voices from his mind, tries
to remember the great round world
outside these walls, the color
and fragrance of summer, the sky at dawn,

but all he can hear is the thunder
of voices around him, a dozen
stories at once, boxing him in.
He wants to give shape to a story
that will leave these people silent,
amazed, a story they'll tell
over and over, after he's gone.
His story will be about his leaving,
and they'll listen so carefully
they won't hear him go out the door
or run across the wet summer grass.

—for Larry Levis

Vicious

Alone in a room watching it snow.
Standing still at the window
for an hour or more, pacing the room
twice, trying to not presume

too much, though snow presumes to fall
in autumn, its whiteness droll
in its recollection of how clean
we were before we were mean,

nasty, Sid and Nancy in bed
in the Chelsea, being led
from their room as it swayed and burned,
the last bridge, then he turned

against her, a half-turn really, half
toward himself. And he laughed.
Why does falling snow bring this to mind?
Sid, you got out just in time,

before the snow could cover things up,
before you were old, poor, tough.
You didn't have to take Nancy too.
Or maybe you did: Her: You.

Velvet Rope

Just what goes on in this cartoon?
The sky is brown, the earth is blue,
the clothes they wear are ripped,
the words they say make no sense,
which makes it all too difficult,
hard to like and harder to know.

The world's a place I'd like to know
a little better, not like cartoons
remembered vaguely, difficult
for no good reason, wind that blows
the birch tree over makes no sense,
no spring is here, no come to grips.

I think I've had enough of gripes,
this tripe that only hollers NO,
this rambling trying to make sense,
as American as cartoons,
their colors red white blue,
flag of what is difficult.

Why not join a different cult,
one that uses different tropes,
believes the color of love is blue,
wears silk pants because they know
it's sticky in Khartoum,
crazy with color, alive with scents.

What you say may not make sense
to everyone, words culled
from the fevers of popular tunes,
your sense of humor a rope
you dangle before them, *no*
for their *yes*, pop for their blues.

What have you got to lose?
A world made of nonsense,
people you'd rather not know,
members of another cult,
wrapped inside their velvet rope,
hoping their guitars are tuned.

Stay tuned for a grope in next week's
strip, a cold and knowing glance—
all you'll lose is fifty cents.

—*for Kevin Gilbert*

Train

Train skims fields like a low-flying
plane, dusting the crops with poison,
looking for the one bad seed.

It runs through woods like a man
after dope, tracks still warm to the touch
of a hand, vibration fading fast.

Train floats through a bog of bones
where voices rise to rancor,
rise from water to the din of air.

What happened there can be felt
on the train, the shudder
of wheels off the track.

Train cuts through rock
where no road goes, no town
lit up for welcome home.

It winds through the night
blue and elastic, finds a way
downhill around curves.

Train skids across the flats
of ice, the word not said,
the thought contained.

It pushes aside what stands
in its way, unless it stands
for something else, metaphor

backward, something big stands for
something small, unimportant
as weeds beside the rail bed.

Frosting

The rain is crooked as it hits the window,
crooked as it falls through the air
of this country—this countryside, I mean,
in which I live with winding roads,
bent trees, corn that follows
the contours of hills home.

The path is dark and narrow, never
straight, it snakes through the wood
with offers of apples and brandy (Hey
old man! You want some candy?).
Clouds in the sky are pentacles,
they number seven and drop the rain
acidly down upon us here—
the way is clear for us to fall, good
fences, good neighbors, good day to die
and good riddance too, nasty old coot.

Brief History

This particular part of the globe knows
its limits but not its boundaries, knows

green grass when it sees it but not
underfoot, under boot, turn it to mud

you can make into bricks and sell
to the country next door, which stores

the bricks until they change color,
mud-brown to blood-red, no one

is dead they're just asleep, now I lay
me, now I peep in the window framed

by bricks in a wall I never climbed,
when all I had was one thin country

and you had three, had to rub them
in my face, didn't you, show me who

was boss hog and who just a pig,
a wide philandering beast of a man,

a flair for pedals to the metal,
a slow disarming way of talking

too loud and too long, so what
went astray when you went away?

A man's country is his castle
you liked to say when you were king

of your beige peninsula, your home
away from your castle, the one made

of bricks filled with mortar and shells,
arms make the man you liked to say

as you picked up a pistol, and, as
if to prove how strong it made you,

put it in your mouth and blew.

Fairy Tale

Here, no one can answer our questions:
How do you know who you are
if you don't use names?

They frown, then smile, then show us
their signatures, loops and dots
forming shapes that live on the page.
It's hard to stop looking, to not
wonder why they can't be pronounced,
or hung in the galleries of *our* city,
where things of beauty are understood.

Like this woman: watch her walk
on by, on air, floating past
like a balloon, with just the right
amount...but she's gone,
and her beauty increases.

Though it's nothing, really,
compared to when she's taken
away and held for a ransom
no one will pay, because
no one knows her name...

Because here there are no names,
only symbols, and the symbol
for her is a circle,
like a balloon, and a dot,

like the hole a bullet makes,
pieces of a balloon
scattered on the floor.

Her death goes unreported here,
though she is beautiful,
and influential, and known
for her signature, which looks
like a breast, or an olive.

And which no one will use
again, as long as this story
is told. Her beauty will always
increase, in the telling,
though other facts will change,
and she will always die
from a bullet.

          If her signature
changes, over the years,
it will happen this way:

          The dot will move out
to join the circle, forming
a ring like a planet's orbit,
spinning gently through the heavens
where no one has a name
                    or ever, ever dies.

River's Edge

Howlin' Wolf howlin' at the moon, full tonight
with lots of light to take us where we want—

a canyon deep, a river green, black tonight
despite the moon, the water cold and fast.

A white moon in green-black water.
A canyon where no people are.

Smell of sage, smell of blood.
The wind that mixes them up

and carries them past, down the river
whose bank we sit on, writ on water

and then drawn over, taken away
to allow for something new,

something borrowed, something green
and blue and gone as you.

What Might Fly Away

Perpendicular across the path
a wild turkey takes its time, head
a yard above the ground, eager
to speak in its nervous way.

Though it can fly, the turkey
chooses to walk when it can, haughty
when it covers ten miles a day.
At sunset it flies up a tree.

It can sleep in any wind, out
of reach of wolf and coyote,
folded over the softest crook.
Then it flies inside the walls of night.

▲
The Way Back
▼

Bright Bird of Weather

Ice from a glacier melts in a glass

Small bird finds a large worm
brown in the brown grass
and lets it go

Birds of a feather lie together

Bright bird of weather
flies circles of warning
warming itself in the air

The air today will be partly clear

Ice plays the mother of water
in a play of the same name
featuring many stars

Birds in the heather mock each other

When you wish upon a star
(who you think you think you are)
you take too much for granted

The night time is the right time

for quiet reflection
the moon your face the water
not a chance for distraction

The low tonight will be in the sixties

Johnny and the Have-Nots
will play loud rock 'n' roll
and pass a hungry hat

The beach wears a yellow hat

I wear mine to protect
from the sun that beats down
like a drum in the sky

The firmament a sonic boom

Cogito ergo zoom
I think therefore I go fast
faster than the night before

Last night's rain set a record

The record spins on the table
the last note echoes over water
c-flat across the flat sea

where no birds fly tonight

The Life of the Mind

She sees sky from his bed, red
above trees that have their own red
no matter the color of sky.

Her green eyes are red, shadowed
the blue of her shoes which led
her through the streets and the night,

out the other side into that
very bed, the sky at this moment
matching her eyes to a cloud.

The cloud stays with her all day.
Before the sun sets, a chance ray
catches the cloud and it's gone,

dissolved into air, a word
spoken aloud but not heard
by anyone but the speaker,

who's forced now to imagine
it's always that way, even when
the story of her life says no.

And *no* is the word on her mind
as she dresses, leaves him behind
in the great green park of her past,

towering trees, grass wild with weeds
unrelated to desire, needs
more red than green at present.

Now: a way out of this mess.
Unless, as they say, there's no rest
for the wicked, no chance to make

those red eyes white again, white
as the snow which colors the night
and those who move in its folds.

Snow covers the green of the park,
for real. She walks until it is dark,
until the sky is something she made up.

She dials a man she doesn't know,
whose car is blue and doesn't show
the rust that eats it from inside.

So much for the life of the mind,
which even at this age declines
all offers of a better life.

The Wonders

The wonders of the modern world
have gathered in a room tonight
to drink a toast to themselves.

The bottles have been stacked in tiers
to resemble stairs that rise
in a column of colorless light

which illuminates the bottles
in a manner which can neither
be forgotten nor described.

All that is known of the light
is that it's more more real by far
than anyone in the room

though its source is a filament
smaller than the veins of their hands,
and more suited to the heat.

Grind the Coffee

Chill of history down the spine.
Cup not full if not a cup.

Many ways to be delinquent.
Watch the planes sail overhead.

Hardscrabble living, no way up.
Mind over matter under the table.

Back in days of hither and yon.
Spin the windmills on the ridge.

Back that hurts from too much wine.
However long the epic goes on.

No excuse for bad equipment.
Grind the coffee is all she said.

Where Are the Thoughts

Words flash, phrases gather and disperse
Sound of the consonant ones
The dialogue public again

What is a sentence if not
A command (says a man)
What is the price of that

Where are the thoughts, a woman
Asks, those beyond consumption
Where can they be found

What has been decided, asks
Another, when will this be over,
Can I go home yet?

Not until you think, says
Someone offstage, off
The page the crowd is on

▲ ▲ ▲

Not a thought between us
On the corduroy couch
As the night takes control

No thoughts outside
Where birds at the feeder
Fight over something unseen

Not a bow or a quiver
Or an arrow to shoot
A hole in a missing thought

Not a thought for the others,
The missing marauders
In search of lethal faith

▲   ▲   ▲

Someone in a club has stolen
My ideas, says the song, says
The man in the grey lawsuit

Standing at my door in the rain
Singing a terrible dirge
Of half-formed thoughts

Known as the law,
Which stands for order
But proves a maze...

He says it's too late
His client thought it first
The law stands against me

▲   ▲   ▲

I am pressed into its wall
Pushed too hard and long
Into the unforgiving surface

A surfeit of emotions pushes out
Hernias of the calm facade
Little angels of thought

Singing hymns as I leave
Out the door marked Enter
In metal-flake spray paint

The subway has no answers
For as long as I ride
I decide to go deeper

The canary in the mine
Becoming the air
Unbecoming the mind

▲ ▲ ▲

The car stops, releases
Its riders below the storm
Raging above, looking for doves

Finding hate on the street
It floods the sidewalks
The natives call it water

And let it wash over them
Oblivious to any law
That says otherwise

Says stop it right there
And listen to me
I know what you think

Before you think it, I
Won't go away so hand
Over your black and white

Life, let me color it in:
Green for envy, blue for the sky
Far from your open hands

▲ ▲ ▲

Where are the thoughts that
Come with age, unengaged
To racing hearts in cars

Wind in the face of willows
Yellow bugs on the screen
Drowning the golden voice

How do thoughts talk if not
Words yet, just sounds
In the air around our heads

Wail of the cat, screech of
The tire, erase the thought—
Drive the damp night

Under stars of rumination,
Galactic intrusions, legions
Of myth connecting dots

▲ ▲ ▲

Funny how one thought
Leads nowhere, another
Goes straight to the point

Of light in the ceiling,
Feeling filtered down
In swirls of warm tones

That begin as faint music
Then pillory the senses,
Reflecting what is there

Instead of what is not,
A dot on the page
That says stop.

Natalia

The slide in the park shines under the moon.
She sees it but goes to the creek

nearby, silver and cold, running downhill
for a mile before it flattens and stops

above the dam, no longer a creek
but something made, frozen shore to shore.

She leaves the park and walks in a field,
moon on the snow lighting her way.

The snow is as light as her hair.
It flies up from her feet as she walks,

making clouds that follow her briefly
before falling back to themselves.

She sees that the moon is not in its place.
Snow settles around her when she stops

and tries to recall where it should be:
on the far side of the sky,

that vacant spot between the stars
which must be filled so she can sleep.

Forty Words for Fear

The snow is as blue as the sky was
before the clouds that held the snow
were formed, blue as it is now.

The sun shines down to melt it
but trees block the way.
Blue in the shadows, it stays.

The blue is what we're after,
the high above, the here below,
the cold news we have to know.

Flocks of flakes big as birds
change the plans we made.
We don't fly south. We stay.

We shovel it, we make a path.
We follow the path to the woods,
but cannot find the road.

The road would lead us out,
though all we need is here.
We have forty words for fear.

Confluence

How the snow melts to keep this river flowing
when it's this cold, New England dead of winter,
is as far beyond me as the headwaters
of either stream that joins the other
in this valley. The river the streams form
rises and falls, lives in a bed,
has a mouth that tells how it feels
to wear sand and stone on one side,
the light of day on the other.

The Way Back

The sound the form the way it is
the way the bricks climb the wall
to form the building where we sit
making sounds with words we found

The sound the beat the way it was
the pounding from within the walls
leaking out to August night
sheen of cars beneath the stars

The bird the worm words not said
pavement wet no tread no tire
dogs that run beside the car
chasing sounds of who you are

The moon the wind the winding road
the way the houses blur
the families inside looking out
purr of engine puff of smoke

The sign the miles ways to go
here to there and then get home
another way through the hills
a road that no one knows

The car the night the radio
the songs that make you young
what they shine on there and there
seen at last for what they mean

The sound the light the way to be
the music driving into night
notes from somewhere coming on
telling stories of the road

The lost the found the in between
the place we find ourselves
and now the room the fire lit
sleep to take us way back home

Wyn Cooper was raised in Michigan, and educated at the University of Utah and Hollins College. His first book, *The Country of Here Below*, was published in 1987. "Fun," a poem from that collection, was made into Sheryl Crow's Grammy-winning song, "All I Wanna Do," in 1993. The album has since sold over nine million copies, and Cooper has gone on to write songs with David Broza, Bill Bottrell, David Baerwald, and Madison Smartt Bell. After editing *Quarterly West* from 1983 to 1985, Cooper taught at Bennington and Marlboro colleges before turning to writing full time. His poems, stories, essays, and reviews have appeared in *Ploughshares*, *Agni*, *Verse*, *Antioch Review*, *Harvard Magazine*, *Fence*, and more than fifty other magazines. His poems are included in eight anthologies of contemporary poetry, and he has given readings across the country. He lives in Vermont.

Author photo: Susan Lippman

AMERICAN POETRY FROM WHITE PINE PRESS

THE WAY BACK
Wyn Cooper
4 pages $14.00 paper

THE CARTOGRAPHER'S TONGUE
Susan Rich
108 pages $14.00 paper

TROUBLE IN HISTORY
David Keller
94 pages $14.00 paper
Winner 1999 White Pine Press Poetry Prize

THE FLOATING ISLAND
Pablo Medina
104 pages $14.00 paper

WINGED INSECTS
Joel Long
96 pages $14.00 paper
Winner 1998 White Pine Press Poetry Prize

IN THE PINES: LOST POEMS 1972-1997
David St. John
224 pages $16.00 paper

A GATHERING OF MOTHER TONGUES
Jacqueline Joan Johnson
116 pages $12.00 paper
Winner 1997 White Pine Press Poetry Prize

PRETTY HAPPY!
Peter Johnson
96 pages $12.00 paper

BODILY COURSE
Deborah Gorlin
90 pages $12.00 paper
Winner 1996 White Pine Press Poetry Prize

TREEHOUSE: NEW & SELECTED POEMS
William Kloefkorn
224 pages $15.00 paper

CERTAINTY
David Romtvedt
96 pages $12.00 paper

ZOO & CATHEDRAL
Nancy Johnson
80 pages $12.00 paper
Winner 1995 White Pine Press Poetry Prize

DESTINATION ZERO
Sam Hamill
184 pages $15.00 paper
184 pages $25.00 cloth

CLANS OF MANY NATIONS
Peter Blue Cloud
128 pages $14.00 paper

HEARTBEAT GEOGRAPHY
John Brandi
256 pages $15.00 paper

LEAVING EGYPT
Gene Zeiger
80 pages $12.00 paper

WATCH FIRE
Christopher Merrill
192 pages $14.00 paper

BETWEEN TWO RIVERS
Maurice Kenny
168 pages $12.00 paper

TEKONWATONTI: MOLLY BRANT
Maurice Kenny

DRINKING THE TIN CUP DRY
William Kloefkorn
87 pages $8.00 paper

GOING OUT, COMING BACK
William Kloefkorn
96 pages $11.00 paper

JUMPING OUT OF BED
Robert Bly
48 pages $7.00 paper

WHY NOT
Joel Oppenheimer
46 pages $7.00 paper

TWO CITIZENS
James Wright
48 pages $8.00 paper

SLEEK FOR THE LONG FLIGHT
William Matthews
80 pages $8.00 paper
WHY I CAME TO JUDEVINE
David Budbill
72 pages $7.00 paper

AZUBAH NYE
Lyle Glazier
56 pages $7.00 paper

SMELL OF EARTH AND CLAY
East Greenland Eskimo Songs
38 pages $5.00 paper

FINE CHINA: TWENTY YEARS OF EARTH'S DAUGHTERS
230 pages $14.00 paper

Poetry in Translation from White Pine Press

THE CITY AND THE CHILD
Ales Debeljak
68 pages $14.00

PERCHED ON NOTHING'S BRANCH
Selected Poems of Attila Joszef
104 pages $14.00

WINDOWS THAT OPEN INWARD
Poems by Pablo Neruda, Photographs by Milton rogovin
96 pages $20.00

HEART OF DARKNESS
Ferida Durakovic
112 pages $14.00

AN ABSENCE OF SHADOWS
Marjorie Agosin
128 pages $15.00

HEART'S AGONY
SELECTED POEMS OF CHIHA KIM
128 PAGES $14.00

THE FOUR QUESTIONS OF MELANCHOLY
Tomaz Salamun
224 pages $15.00

A GABRIELA MISTRAL READER
232 pages $15.00

ALFONSINA STORNI: SELECTED POEMS
72 pages $8.00

CIRCLES OF MADNESS: MOTHERS OF THE PLAZA DE MAYO
Marjorie Agosín
128 pages $13.00   Bilingual

SARGASSO
Marjorie Agosín
92 pages $12.00   Bilingual

THE STONES OF CHILE
Pablo Neruda
98 pages $10.00   Bilingual

VERTICAL POETRY: RECENT POEMS BY ROBERTO JUARROZ
118 pages $11.00   Bilingual

LIGHT AND SHADOWS
Juan Ramon Jimenez
70 pages $9.00

ELEMENTAL POEMS
Tommy Olofsson
70 pages $9.00

FOUR SWEDISH POETS:
STROM, ESPMARK, TRANSTROMER, SJOGREN
131 pages $9.00

NIGHT OPEN
Rolf Jacobsen
221 pages $15.00

SELECTED POEMS OF OLAV HAUGE
92 pages $9.00

TANGLED HAIR
Love Poems of Yosano Akiko
48 pages $7.50 paper   Illustrated

A DRIFTING BOAT
An Anthology of Chinese Zen Poetry
200 pages $15.00

BETWEEN THE FLOATING MIST
Poems of Ryokan
88 pages $12.00

WINE OF ENDLESS LIFE
Taoist Drinking Songs
60 pages $9.00

TANTRIC POETRY OF KUKAI
80 pages $7.00

ABOUT WHITE PINE PRESS

Established in 1973, White Pine Press is a non-profit publishing house dedicated to enriching our literary heritage; promoting cultural awareness, understanding, and respect; and, through literature, addressing social and human rights issues. This mission is accomplished by discovering, producing, and marketing to a diverse circle of readers exceptional works of poetry, fiction, non-fiction, and literature in translation from around the world. Through White Pine Press, authors' voices reach out across cultural, ethnic, and gender boundaries to educate and to entertain.

To insure that these voices are heard as widely as possible, White Pine Press arranges author reading tours and speaking engagements at various colleges, universities, organizations, and bookstores throughout the country. White Pine Press works with colleges and public schools to enrich curricula and promotes discussion in the media. Through these efforts, literature extends beyond the books to make a difference in a rapidly changing world.

As a non-profit organization, White Pine Press depends on support from individuals, foundations, and government agencies to bring you important work that would not be published by profit-driven publishing houses. Our grateful thanks to the many individuals who support this effort as Friends of White Pine Press and to the following organizations: Amter Foundation, Ford Foundation, Korean Culture and Arts Foundation, Lannan Foundation, Lila Wallace-Reader's Digest Fund, Margaret L. Wendt Foundation, Mellon Foundation, National Endowment for the Arts, New York State Council on the Arts, Trubar Foundation, Witter Bynner Foundation, the Slovenian Ministry of Culture, The U.S.-Mexico Fund for Culture, and Wellesley College.

Please support White Pine Press' efforts to present voices that promote cultural awareness and increase understanding and respect among diverse populations of the world. Tax-deductible donations can be made to:

White Pine Press
P.O. Box 236, Buffalo, NY 14201